Graffiti Calculus

Graffiti Calculus

A Poem by Mary-Sherman Willis

CW Books

Published by CW Books
P.O. Box 541106
Cincinnati, OH 45254-1106

ISBN: 9781625490568
LCCN: 2013953469

Poetry Editor: Kevin Walzer
Business Editor: Lori Jareo

Visit us on the web at http://www.readcwbooks.com.

Cover design: Rebecca Woods
Author photograph: Mary Noble Ours

Acknowledgments

My profound thanks go to Katherine McNamara and Artist's Proof Editions for publishing the excerpted chapbook *Caveboy* as an illustrated art book in collaboration with my son, who designed and produced it, and as an iBook for iPad.

Thanks also to the editors of magazines in which parts of this book have appeared: *The Southern Poetry Review* ("The Phenomenology of the Name"); *The Cortland Review* (portions of "Kilroy").

My deep gratitude goes to the MacDowell Foundation for the time to work on these poems. And to teachers and friends like Mark Jarman, Claudia Emerson, David McAleavey, Patrick Donnelly, Bruce Snider, Eavan Boland, Eleanor Wilner, Terese Svoboda, Mary Stewart Hammond, Naomi Guttman, Alex Pierce, Patricia Corbus, Katherine McNamara, Sylvie McNamara, and Martha Carlson-Bradley for their support and attention to this manuscript.

And to Scott, Camille, and Collin, my love.

A child said, What is the grass? . . .
I guess it is a uniform hieroglyphic . . .

—Walt Whitman

Contents

The Phenomenology of the Name

1.

In the beginning was your name, which we gave you to make you
      a part of us and apart from us.

As with our DNA, we fixed our own names in you; from your name
      you derived your tag, CONE:

You, consonantally slurred; a graff writer's nom de paint stick,
      nom de Krylon, de Rusto Fat Cap.

You, ice cream's cornucopia, woman's breast, traffic barrier, dunce hat,
      a spray nozzle, the bowl of a bong.

You, who exist in the dimensional world, a piece of solid geometry
      steady on its base or a hollow funnel.

And you, an experiment in phenomenology. I parsed and puzzled it.
      You explained, it's C-plus-ONE:

your first initial plus you, unique. Or rather, The One. See One.
      See me. Or, don't see me.

2.

When you were home, how well could I see you? My body radio-tuned
    to your foot-thud up the stairs,

the floor-creak overhead, your desk chair's wheel-rumble, speakers'
    gangsta-thump, I felt your presence

on my skin, but you were a blur to me. I may have been blind, but not
    uninformed. Our doors were open to you.

I had my own sneaking-around girlhood to dwell on. I paid attention.
    Too much attention, you complained.

Hyper-vigilance, a shrink explained. But we believed that at sixteen
    we couldn't keep you

safe at home, or kick you out, yet. I searched your room, "cleaning" it.
    That first experiment

in phenomenology quickly yielded up your stash, but spooked me less
    than the vodka on your breath.

3.

In the parable, as the father sat waiting for his prodigal boy to return
     to him, the mother surely

did not sequester herself in the tent, carving a hole in her heart.
     You were avoiding home

and so began my hunt for you, to know who you were, inhaling
     and tasting. Not just looking

but seeing. Like a cat attuned to the quick odd movement, a dog
     nosing the trail, a dancer

stepping to her partner, I was a mother vibrating through the city
     to your telling absence.

It's not enough to say, *if only I could give my angels charge over you
     lest you dash your foot against a stone.*

I had to find you. You had left your marks, first on my body, my heart,
     and now on the city itself.

4.

I leashed the dog and walked the streets looking for your tag. *Intentionality*
proceeds from the subject, said Heidegger.

I (the subject) walked and looked (predicate) for you (object), or rather
for your tags.

If my intention was to see you, I must let you manifest yourself to me.
Let that which shows itself be seen

from itself in the very way in which it shows itself, from itself, he said.
And now I saw you all around me:

your tags on walls, the sidewalk, light posts, curbs I'd never noticed.
Like Hansel's pebbles, they wended

in a line from home, down the streets and alleys of Dupont Circle
as if to tease me, to show me the way

you went, what you could do without me, how I could not stop you.
Or were they to lead you home?

5.

Calculus, Latin for *pebble*, a chip off the old block tumbled over
time and distance.

On the gridded sidewalk each step is an integer. *Step on a crack,
break your mother's back.* Step,

drop a pebble. Step, here was the calculus of you moving away
from me, each of us an entity, yet linked.

Here was your motion and rate of change, and here my continuity,
and this my paradox:

if every step I took brought me halfway to you, how many steps
must I take to reach you?

What was my limit, where we converged as a function of time?
The textbook says, *for any fixed*

*standard of accuracy, you can always be sure to be within that limit,
provided you have gone far enough.*

6.

The height of a child as he grows over time is a continuous function.
        It was I, the notcher and the dater

on the doorframe through which you came and went; I, the datakeeper,
        demonstrator (*see how tall?*)

for whom the top notch would become a reach, a stretch; I through
        whom you came, then went,

who built my back and biceps lifting you, tickled *I'm coming to get you!*
        I developed a taste for a burden,

for your arms ever-reaching. Now my arms looped your waist,
        your chin on my head.

I was reduced to beck and call at the door. The graph of a continuous
        function can be drawn

without lifting the chalk from the board. Did you think that you
        and I were through?

7.

All around me the family crouched low to the ground, elbowing
      under barbwire, gunfire.

Your father hid at work. Your sister went outbacking beyond reach
      with some Brits and a German,

counting the flies at Ayers' Rock, the crocs in the ditches, koalas
      in the ghost gums—the miles

an irksome blur. Every few months she'd call home breezily, telling us
      her new phenomenology:

songlines across the red desert, the Dreaming that names the world
      into being, a secret campsite

she'd stumbled upon, its occult stone paintings. Into the phone I poured
      my own songline: *But where are you?*

If you died, where would I begin to look for you? A sniper circled D.C.
      We waited to be mugged by death.

8.

Terror telegraphs itself. That first night you stayed away from home
       the dog placed his moist jowls

on the bed as I roiled in the dark. The silent house was sucking
       all the oxygen and I lay gasping.

I had been calling your cellphone, stabbing a tattoo to conjure you,
       to call you back to quarters.

Once, you answered. My voice left my throat and flew to my limits,
       transmuting in the air into a fist

to hold you there. You disconnected me. Now, my hearing was like
       the dog's, agitating at the door before

the key is in, listening for its opening motif, its closing a bomb
       I would have welcomed.

Terror leads to terror, now I know. But that . . . that was true vertigo,
       to feel in motion even when at rest.

9.

You moved through streets of men, a boy earning his manhood making
   his display of risk. Making his name.

To make your name, you crafted a cipher in the hand of a non-entity,
   a zero, a ghost among us dropping traces.

A vandal's hand to cops, to me. To you, a code for the cognoscenti,
   your fellow prodigals, squanderers

who roamed lamplit streets, listening to the city's stone walls call
   OBEY . . . NARS . . . KOMA . . . BORF . . .

COOL "DISCO" DAN . . . FELON . . . CERT . . . KAOS . . . and hissing
   your own clatter babble:

click-a click-a click-a . . . *pfsss pfsssss* . . . exposing your back to the street
   as if in private, pissing.

You vaporized and were reborn in a mist of adrenaline and paint fumes,
   as No One; NONE; N-plus-ONE . . .

Kilroy

10.

In my Cold War duck-and-cover American girlhood, in the bull's-eye
of Washington's nuclear radius,

under a blue sky etched in contrails and filled by day with keening
air emergency sirens, in brick-walled

Horace Mann Elementary, Mrs. Wilson drew her chalk across the board.
Let AB be a line segment with midpoint M.

*Let two small semicircles X and Y rise above AB; a parabola Z below AB;
and a large semicircle L, above X and Y . . .*

And I doodled this charm: now let two little eyeballs fill X and Y! And
two sets of cartoon fingertips below AB!

Printed *KILROY WAS HERE.* And because I could: let *AB* become the
horizon of the whole Earth,

flexing along lines of longitude and latitude from sea to shining sea. Hail
Empire's wandering warrior, king killer . . .

11.

He was Kilroy, Super-GI, all-present all-seeing. Like God. There first
    to greet advancing men on rubble

at blood-soaked beachheads, on shattered battlements, his face and
    name daubed on still-smoking walls.

Kilroy was here. The peeping imp kept a step ahead of American troops
    from Europe to the Pacific.

He was there at Potsdam, when Stalin came back from the toilet asking,
    Who is this Kilroy?

A year later, safety-suited, Geiger-countered Blandy found him on the
    nuked SS *New York*'s port side

as clouds of sand and shattered coral rained Strontium-90 from the sky
    onto Bikini Atoll.

Natives on Kwajalein, sucking Lucky Strikes and bottles of Coke,
    goggle-watched two sunrises that day.

12.

Kilroy is back. He's bombing walls, destroying, killing train cars, busting
       and ex-ing tags, sidebusting throw-ups,

dropping and burning pieces. He's on maneuver, alone or mustered
       in a crew, with his cans of ammo,

his digital intel. He finds his spot, cuts his lines fast and with precision,
       an insurgent dodging cops and thugs.

He's a hardcore free agent, straight-edge or into 40s and cigarettes,
       into hip-hop, into go-go, into punk,

into guns. He's an upstart, a raider, a thief—*steal paint, steal the wall*—
       a commando outlaw ninja samurai,

locked and loaded, with his uncontrollable urge to get up and wreck
       every wall in sight. Every underpass

and overpass, sidewalk, billboard, subway, train-yard, toilet booth,
       garbage-stinking alleyway is his.

13.

The wall knows itself to be inexhaustible and endlessly renewable.
      It brings us Kilroy, sizzling through

cathode ray tubes, LEDs, computer screens, flatscreens, jumbotrons
      with the ping and zip of electrons.

He comes to us (even as the screens reflect us), and speaks to us
      in the first person of the brand.

He wants to be of service, flapping tongues of cash, setting our
      coordinates, helping us decide

what to buy. Coins and bills course from his fingertips: currency:
      the circulation of a name.

And Kilroy is there, screaming through space on a unilinear subway,
      logo turned logorrhea.

It's the wall upon which to leave the free stroke of the name,
      the same story over and over.

14.

I follow you, pebble-dropper, to learn what lasts beyond the heart
  and body, to read the walls' stories.

You are the writer, I am the reader. The walls say Kilroy was just a man,
  a warship riveter who chalked his mark

on each steel hull he touched (each *she*) and launched his name
  as a brand of American empire.

Like a virus, a whispered rumor, lip-to-lip and hand-to-hand, he moves
  among us despite himself.

A raindrop on dry ground becomes a roaring flood, unstoppable.
  Kilroy passes through

the walls of any city like a Bedouin driving his flocks and bundles,
  no matter who is king.

Whatever the allurements or threats of a kingdom, he can slip back
  into the desert to await better times.

15.

First, the innocence of birth, says the wall. Kilroy sits in the Garden
        knowing only his Father the King,

the shady apple tree and peace. How long before he'd tire of all that?
        There is that wall. And so

the Fall; shame; pain. He hits the streets, a willing nomad. Not for him
        the plagues of a ruined Eden,

the besieged city, the pile of skulls. Consider a tribe of nomad Kilroys
        being nurtured by a King

into an army primed to fight for him. But now his troops are restless
        and goad him into battle.

How does a King draw back his nomads inside the wall and keep them
        loyal? Sell them stuff. Make them want it.

Bog them down with what they cannot carry. Or hold, like freedom.
        Then send them off to war.

16.

Or this legend: the Hero on his Road of Trials. Kilroy, an ambitious boy,
    travels to distant lands

where a King's monster rakes its fiery breath across forest and field.
    Kilroy draws his sword from his thigh

and practicing parries and feints, calculates his promised reward:
    the princess; the treasure; the land;

but most importantly, *so importantly*, fame. For twelve years he voyages
    hither and thither on trivial errands

to placate the King's beast, filling out forms, writing reports, completing
    inscrutable tests.

At each ordeal, he chalks up mark after mark. The King is *disappointed*
    every time, and turns up the heat.

Burned, Kilroy unsheathes the sword, takes aim at his tormentor,
    and true to his name, kills the King.

17.

So now, fatherless Kilroy does his pimp-walk ghetto-dance, with daps
and high-fives for his crew.

He ascends his house-stoop to revisit his past of heroic poverty,
key to his brand.

We observe the pocked and cracked plaster, the window overlooking
an air shaft, stained walls

exuding meals cooked without ventilation, unwashed bedding.
Distant gunfire, screams, sirens.

He sings of his Moms, his queen-consort who hunts him with all
her broken heart.

What to do with her? Let her wander a vast and empty palace,
and look at the walls.

You must kill a thing to know it, Kilroy tells his crew. *Then you become it.*
Glory to King Kilroy!

18.

The wall is a mirror waiting for a mark. Rauschenberg took an eraser
    to a drawing by de Kooning,

signed his own name to it, then sold it. I think of you, buffing your
    own tag as punishment.

Photographing it first. I think of Plato's cave, its walls knotted up with
    the tension of learning to spell.

From the heart of the Bronx, walls erupted into a jungle of ego creepers.
    Inflorescences bloomed

on decayed institutions, prisonlike projects, on huckstering billboards
    by the sides of throughways

that sever neighborhoods. Everywhere, boys in molt circulated their tags
    like fungus-flung spores,

martyring themselves to the ghetto. Angels of a new aesthetic
    or cavepainters calling up the beast?

Paleoboy

19.

The wall is our shepherd. It brings us to green pastures and leads us
        by still waters to the cave,

before men made walls, when wooded gullies fingered open savannas
        veined by networks of game trails;

when people were kept on the move by the lumbering mammoth,
        the tiger's cat tang, the yipping wolf.

Isolated bands of men with spears, women with carry baskets, sifted
        through dappled shadows,

children idling alongside, toddlers riding their uncles' shoulders,
        babies rolled and slung in pelts.

On frozen plains, herds of ibex or bison or shaggy stiff-maned horses
        were driven like dry leaves

in a steppe wind, a thin orthography of clouds in the blue above them,
        hunter and hunted.

20.

Camped in oak shade near a cliff ledge sits the Boy, teenaged, bent
        this late summer afternoon

over a flint shard he's learning to knap, deftly torqueing its scalloped
        edge sharp against a pebble,

flakes shimmering around his bare feet. A bearded youth sits nearby,
        showing him how. Their long hair,

hacked short in front, smells of wood smoke and boy-funk. Red ocher
        stripes and dots their skin,

but flies are drawn to soot-inked cuts on the Boy's arms and shoulders.
        He swats them, swats at his eyes,

and moves closer to the fire and its sweet smoke. His mother comes,
        rising from a squat, a clay bowl in hand.

She bends to him, fingers dipped in green mash to daub the wounds.
        Meat sizzles on the bone.

21.

Meat sizzles on the bone. Eyeing him, fluent in his signs of need,
    she sees like a crow

that teases wisps into a nest of care around him. She admires his
    hands shaping the blade—

how quickly he learns—glad to send him out armed and make
    a hunter of him. She has dreamed

of him in the cave, its hissing silence, the stars snuffed out. A place
    she'd known well, where crow-eye

becomes dull; where the she-bear, a hunter who knows to crouch
    with her back to the wind, deep

in her own fur, also slashes blade-clawed; also snuffs roots with grit
    in her teeth. She would not be

the first mother to lose her child to the underworld's song. She would
    have to dream him back.

22.

Five set out from camp at dawn, a hunting party, the Boy among them,
        trotting single-file along

a game trail through scrubby bottomland, up a grassy ridge high
        in purple thistles and twiggy forbs

that burr their clothes. The air is sharp. Somewhere a finch trills,
        a woodpecker drums a tree,

pine needles comb the breeze, but they don't hear. The practiced eldest,
        bone-tipped spear in hand,

kneels to show wild-dog scat, tinged blue with berries, threaded with
        the bones and fur of mice, *fresh.*

All hungry attention, they see the grass flattened by the bedded herd;
        the ground scuffed by rooting pigs

at the base of an oak; the deer's print—there!—where it turned to look,
        the glistening red drops . . .

23.

The Boy's been perched at the crotch of this sappy pine since the band
  split and sent him sprinting off alone

into the forest, taking a shortcut to where the game trail crosses a creek
  in the bottom of a ravine.

His eye followed the eloquent chevrons pocked into soft earth,
  to read living meaning:

a doe pausing to graze, working her sensitive lips; a buck's four-square
  planted stance, his thick neck

lofting his crowned head; a scramble of fawns, their snorting play,
  hightailing to their mothers.

Then nothing, no scuffed needles, bent twig; no blood. Fresh wind rocks
  the treetops. He studies

their swaying awhile, imagines himself a cricket riding a blade of grass.
  Outside of time, his senses roar.

24.

Cracking branches make a burst of hollow explosions behind him
        in the pillared dark. The Boy turns

to scan for a presence in the emptiness between the trees, to see deep
        into the forest for movement,

for the deeper blackness of the animal. He hears his own breath
        whistle in his nose, and quiets it.

He is willing the beast to come to him, to allow it to manifest itself to him
        by calling it up, part

by part: oh wide-set leaflike ears, oh oak-brown nose glossy as river-rock,
        oh sapling-thin legs,

oh white tail—so that when the snuffling and coughing, when the clatter
        of dry leaves kicked,

the head held low, pink foam at the mouth—when the Boy sees the
        animal at last, it's familiar.

25.

The Boy stops, locks. Not even his hair, braided and tied with catgut, stirs.
    Off to the right, a jot, a flicker

in twig-scribble: another boy crouches, steps catlike over ground fern,
    gripping an antler-tipped pike.

A third boy stands up to the left and behind the animal, spear raised.
    But the doe, dragging a shaft in the neck,

turns and offers her flank to the Boy. She is his. With dread and desire,
    somehow he springs

from the tree—hands shaking, body tingling—somehow launches
    his weapon, hears the thump

of a chest hit, and the scene shatters into a thousand shards of sense—
    the thrash of boys and beast

to hold her down, to pierce, to slice her throat, a gargled cry, the tongue,
    pools of warm blood. Her eyes.

26.

Only after the opening and taking apart of the doe—the handing out
       of the stout muscle of her heart,

spongy lungs, sleek brown liver, the reeking gut—can the Boy release
       into hunger. He is ravenous.

They pack their trophy out of the forest in a hum of flies and wasps,
       shadowed by buzzards.

The guts they throw to skulking dogs. He cracks hazelnuts in his teeth
       and chews as he walks.

That night, flames flutter on hissing wood. He is licking his fingers over
       and over: gratitude is hunger satisfied.

When a girl crawls under his fur, he makes his hands soft to touch her.
       Crickets agitate the air. A big cat groans

and parents rise to scan the dark for eyes, to reach for their children
       to hold them close to the body.

27.

The body is walled territory while it stands. While asleep, defenseless.
To invade a body, seek out

the openings in the bodywall, marked by the appetites. The Boy fingers
woad-inked creatures

up the ridge of her spine, the dot circlets of her breasts, her clan mark
striping her chin,

mapping her as she arches her neck to him and shows him the signs.
His sensory vents wide,

he presses himself to open her up, just as he opens to risk. A girl's risk:
to put her body under siege,

then await delivery, death's blade. To become a wall transected
by the life spasm inside her.

There was no mother-pain for which she was not prepared; for now,
she's aware of its telling absence.

28.

Now the Boy sleeps (at the dawn of human dreaming, at the center
    of his own dream) and replays

the day's images on the cave of his skull in ochers, greens and blues:
    he and the girl share meat,

she opening her mouth for him, red and glossy. He strokes her bare
    shoulder, gilded with fireglow,

her throat and cheekbones. Her loose hair curled in a snaky nimbus,
    she slithers under the skin.

The fire flares. In his dream the Boy looks down to see the breathing doe
    curled at his feet like a dog.

Dew cools his sleeping brow; his body's lax—but for his heart thudding,
    his chest rising and falling

in spite of himself and his restless eyes. A dog growls and woofs in its
    own dreams, twitching.

29.

His dream is a story, its threads weaving above their sleeping heads,
    the hunters and the hunted.

It is spring in the dream, the thawed ground moist and printable
    under a scrim of low plants. Late sun

reveals the facts slantwise: tracks in a trail with which he is at pains
    to communicate. In the chatter

of twig and leaf, the doe is telling him she's a doe, her rear tracks
    to the outside of the front ones,

loping comfortably—he feels the muscles of her flank in his own
    loose-hipped ease,

the flick of her up-cocked tail in his steps. The air streaming
    through his flared nostrils

is the same air filling hers, a waterway riffling pebbles, telling
    a new story.

30.

In his dream the Boy knows, *It's easy. I am made for this, wing-footed,*
    crow-eyed as she taught me,

croaking mark *and* mark *and* mark. The trail sings to him, preparing him
    for the next mark.

All line and pattern: the linnet's oscillating starts and stops above
    swaying grasses, fern-spiral,

the sinuous willow fringed with green blades, the horse's arched neck,
    the otter diving for river fish:

lines and points in motion. But then a novelty along the way: a nipped
    stem, tufts of snagged winter fur,

the odd thing in the path, the broken pattern catching his eye. Suddenly
    he stops: seed-studded bear scat,

coiled at his feet! Alone, shivering, his dream-naked body raked with
    fear . . . Where are his knife and spear?

31.

From where the Boy stands, the sunny plain rolls behind and away
       in mazy vagueness; in front

the trail leads directly into shadowy forest. He dream-fidgets, peering
       deep into the darkness

as the thrill of risk surges in him—is he not the fastest, the canniest
       of trackers? A breeze raises

the hair on his arms. He snuffs the air: pine, fern, moss, wet leaves.
       A gap in the trees' sentinel trunks

opens to him. With it comes a warning scent, meaty, musky; a scent
       of shit and carrion and fruit.

But he's picked up her track again, the doe whose prints were not
       the beginning of counting or writing

but of storytelling—a story he was rehearsing when he looks up
       and sees the cave.

The Limit

32.

I chased your shadow to the limits of my map of D.C., tracking you
      along the snaking Red Line

from Glenmont to Shady Grove. My body was weak with dread.
      Behind Union Station I saw

your face lit by a flame; at L'Enfant Plaza, your mouth at the mouth
      of a squat bottle; your hand

fingering another hand in Brookland, slipping something into a pocket;
      back sliding down a wall,

head-loll in Brentwood; eyes rolled to white, drifting half-shut, flicking
      open in Fort Totten;

breath slowing in Friendship Heights, lips huffing. Or home in Dupont,
      you, sleeping like a fevered child.

Was that really you, or some other woman's son? What part was me,
      at the limit at which we converged?

33.

It was my own fault. I'd showed you dark parts of the city to scare you
      a little. That man walking funny

on Columbia Road, vomit on his shirt: *That's what happens when you.*
      The brawl on the Mall

under July 4 fireworks, a skull thud on pavement, blood leaking:
      That's because they.

These little vials on our street. Those needles in the bushes: *See?*
      They're from people who.

Stand still, let me show you. Wandering Tommy's sad stories? *All lies.*
      Look at his arms.

The Bag Princess living on our sidewalk, haughty in designer castoffs:
      Put coins in a rattled cup,

but don't bring them home. We had enough, at home, of appetites amok!
      For godsake, don't be like that.

34.

Code Orange, baby!—snarling Granddad's sloshing bourbon on the rug!
    Grandma's in tears. Alert! Alert!

Uncle Brother's looking to score on M Street, babies on board; Code Red!
    Homeland Security!

Auntie Sister's doing lines in the bathroom, bottle of Jack under the
    bed . . . We're on lockdown!

What's in that box? Behind that mirror? In these pockets, that glass, that
    purse, that cockeyed face, the eyes,

the mouth — *all* appetites running amok! Battlements smoke across
    the Potomac, snipers roam the malls,

anthrax in the mail, a drydrunk emperor struts the decks—all systems
    normal. Every day, a new sun rises,

birdsong across the land. At Al-Anon: *my name is . . . and I am . . .* the same
    story over and over.

35.

In the house's closed system, we pinged against each other unpredictably,
     glittering flecks held in suspension.

When you were gone, the air prickled our skin. When anyone could be
     anywhere, even an absence

is a presence. The city was an ancient savannah; big cats, dogs in packs
     looking for pattern

and habit. Inside, duty and guilt rooted me in place like some dumb tree,
     as if the best I could do

was to wait for you. I spaded a tidy garden and spoke to it in Latin in a
     fever for order, sharp-bladed

secateurs in hand. *God grant me the serenity.* My fear was to hurt you
     and still I was hurting you.

I locked you out. In the morning I found you in the lilies cradling half
     a gallon of Stoli like a doll.

36.

I locked you out. Your father let you in. He locked you out. I opened up
        the door. You lost your key.

You always lost your key. We kept the door unlocked. We kept the back
        door open; anyone could enter

but not you. You stayed away from home. You stayed inside your room,
        you closed your door.

We knocked. No answer. We barged in but you'd ghosted through the
        walls. When you came home

and I asked you *Where?* and you said *Nowhere* and I asked you *What?*
        and you said *Nothing*

then walked away, that was not even calculus. Just a simple word problem.
        Off with him, said the shrink.

Boot camp, make him suffer. Send him to the desert, to snowy mountains.
        Take away his shoes.

37.

Other mothers hunted their sons alone in the city. We reconnoitered
    in each other's kitchens and told

of sons absconding, leaving only their stink, a memory of their sweet
    heads, soft kisses, their bodies

now only wisps, spinning blue holograms to reach for in the dark.
    Then the calls from school—

he gets up in the middle of class to look out the window; he draws
    on the board while I'm talking;

always late, never there. Get him tested. It became our brand, to have
    a boy we put into a school,

then have to drug to keep him there. The drunk pickups, jail calls,
    the names of lawyers. The meds.

We mouthed *enabling, in denial, intervention, tough love* like pebbles.
    You left me your marks to follow.

38.

Following you I recognized the girl I'd been, out in front of her brothers
        and sisters and heading for

the dark heart of the city. She wore nomad paint, long hair, tribal beads,
        her feet bare. She carried a knife.

Trees dripped sap on the streets in swamp heat. In the marble hives
        of the Capitol, men fomented

conquest, and golden women hummed about them like honeybees.
        The jungles of the empire

were in flames and fire was spreading to the capital. She sought the
        ghetto, something she thought true

and irrevocable to martyr herself to, all else being cons and appetites.
        She sought boys who knew the way in.

What she knew: they rub up against you, then run unencumbered.
        Best to be a boy, she thought.

39.

In the ghetto, Reggie was showing her the way in. They sat on grimy shag
in the haze of incense,

Country Joe on the wall, *Traffic* on the turntable. He passed the joint
and they acted as though

they knew each other. His soft mouth opened like other boys' mouths,
leaving prints that formed

the calculus of her body, marking and walling its limits. Across the city
it was the cocktail hour.

Cicadas revved their motors in the maples above scintillating fireflies
and the *tsk-tsk* of lawn sprinklers.

Men and women slipped their bounds, clinking ice cubes, and the world
seemed to turn on nothing

but the sound. She was figuring out the way. It was a tangled forest; was
a twisty streetscape; was mapless.

40.

She could ape her elders so they would notice her. But they were all
    askew, their works like water,

a fire in the lake. She had her knife and notebook, her hands and eyes.
    Her tribe of boys (like you). Her journey.

It would be epic. 1969, that summer a man put his country's tag on
    the moon. She sat alone in the dark

on a crickety hill in La Honda at the western edge of America, sick
    at the marks he was leaving.

The moon pulsed white above her, the breeze spun ribbons all around,
    the earth rolled and ratcheted below.

She was figuring out how to leave no trace, to ghost about—and not get
    caught. Anywhere at any time,

she could be at the center of a perpetual dream. But when she moved,
    she left you her marks to follow.

The Cave

41.

Daytime, a band of youngsters—six boys, a couple of girls—winds
    single-file through tall grass,

the Boy at the lead. He's taking them to a familiar old campsite
    about a morning's trot away:

the abri of a cave where bears slept in winter. His dream cave. Its mouth
    glows in the sun with ochers,

yellow-orange-red, veined with gray manganese. Down a pebbled slope
    the river sparkles.

The children pick through camp trash—charred sticks, clamshells,
    a chipped bone burin still sharp,

an aurochs's shoulder blade. The Boy chews the end of a twig. Someone
    has painted an ibex on this wall.

He spears it with a slash of charcoal, then makes a spit-slurry of blood-
    red oxide to dab the stone with dots.

42.

The damp cave clay is soft enough to take their prints as they crouch
through a narrow passage at the back.

Flints spark and torches flare into the seasonless black of a cavern
sending arched shadows dancing.

Wet stalactites hang like nippled teats, thick as arms, as glistening guts,
and drip on them.

On chalky yellow walls great beasts rise up: shaggy horned bison, hulking
mammoths with twisting tusks,

horses clattering by on sharp hooves. The children shriek and laugh,
thrilled by their clanging echoes.

Bats squeak and rustle. Ammoniac stink wafts from a void to their left.
They steer clear.

Bear-claw hatchmarks groove the wall; in a corner they find the carcass
of a cub, and they grow quiet.

43.

They clamber deeper down the dropping corridors, snaking slick walls,
    toeing narrow rock ledges

that drop to nothing. Torches flit and glimmer in the columned dark,
    darker than moonless

starless night; than blindness; than death. Fingering the walls, they call
    in the darkness from one to the other.

At the last marking on the stone—the limit of the known trail so far
    and of trail-blazes leading out—

the Boy kneels to palm a mouthful of water from a shallow pool and
    eats a chunk of orange ochre,

chewing the earth with spit. Palm pressed on damp stone, fingers spread
    he sputter-sprays

his hand up to the wrist, then lifts it to admire the stenciled print.
    His toothy grin glows orange.

44.

Soon they're all at it, blowing a dancing field of hand negatives,
       frescoing damp limestone.

Each four fingers and a thumb, each slightly different—one bigger,
       one smaller than the others, an index

or a pinkie bent, a thumb hidden, their fingers V'd with meaning.
       Each his or hers

a name, personal as a body part (*mark* and *mark* and *mark*).
       The chain of hands reaches

down the cave's cool corridor from the past into the future, following
       the earth's own history:

an inland sea's laid-down layers of life, when water flooded dead cells
       with stone and studded the coiled

and folded sediment with fossils. Mark and mark and mark in marble
       veining the soft calcite.

45.

The Boy keeps moving. He feels along a ragged wall and finds a hole
      just wide enough for a child. He's in!

Holding his torch in front, gasping and half-blind with pitch smoke,
      he shimmies and elbows along

a gritty tunnel so tight it crushes his breath. Grimy, elbows and knees
      bloodied, snagged at the waist

by his belted kit bag, it occurs to him like a new idea that he might
      die here!—a thought that propels him,

gulping air, out the hole and down a four-foot drop to the floor
      of a small red chamber.

A pool gleams like tar in the torchlight, absolutely still and silent.
      He shivers in the clammy cold.

Veils of flowstone hang above him. He fingers a moist stalactite
      and opens his bag.

46.

The Boy wants to make an animal, but not child-like, clenching mud
        as his mother had showed him

when she pressed coiled clay to line a basket: *see the lump, the palm-
        and finger-prints? Now make.*

He knew the meat-beasts—horse, deer, aurochs—but not really.
        He hadn't hunted yet.

So he'd made his mother's beast whole from its parts: a snout-face
        with a sharp nose, seedy eyes

and round ears; heavy shoulders and mother-arms for squeezing tight;
        claws and a stump-tail: bear!

Taken from the life by his hand. Container of the bear's living self.
        Talisman; gazing-stock; object of art.

She would fire-heat and harden it to stone for him to carry and keep.
        Even his favorites broke or were lost.

47.

Taken from the life *by his hand*—clay-shaper; toolmaker; spear thrower.
    His hands held dominion

over creatures. And her hand over him, she who had shaped him inside
    her and torn him free of herself.

Then held him, run her thumb on the little teeth in his milk-mouth.
    Then taken the food

from her mouth and fed his gawp. Then wiped him clean of his soil.
    She'd caressed his downy cheek,

as softly as she could with a hard palm. When her hand held his to make
    him stand, he was still her creature.

No one else's. She knew this better than anyone, better even than
    his father would know

who belonged to whom as long as there was life. By making her Boy
    from her life, she left her print in him.

48.

The Boy studies the wall in torchlight flicker. Shifting shadows suggest
        animals and animate

the swells and creases in the damp stone like a dream teasing the image
        from him. He opens himself

to the wall, moving the torch from side to side. At once he sees the doe.
        Above him a crack demarks

her shoulder and back; to the left, her face; fawn speckling on brown,
        her coat. He calls her up

from the base of his spine to his fingers and thinks how to reveal her
        beyond the mark she made.

Is her head down at ease grazing? Is she springing away up-tailed
        with the fleeing herd?

He wants to preserve her—and himself—in a kind of permanent speech
        and for that he needs a line.

49.

He delineates her profile freehand within her limits, etching the stone
        with a burnt stick, the torch

in his other hand. A line flows from the charred tip almost despite him
        and he dances with it

in the solitary darkness, reaching up to the tops of her ear-points,
        crouching low to detail

the delicate front and back legs, their sharp hocks and hooves.
        He fringes the fur of her breast,

belly, scut and tail with golden ocher crayon. The line ends where
        it began and she is embodied.

Then he does the trick he's copied and practiced: two more legs placed
        behind the first. And there she is,

standing *in* the wall. He draws a dark eye and they look at each other,
        the boy and his beast.

50.

The doe steps inside the red chamber, breathing in torchlight,
      flicking her tail. The Boy touches

the stone, hairs on his arms prickling as if his hand might pass
      right through the wall

deep into the earth itself, to safety and home. (Or into emptiness;
      that is the risk!), and body forth

a stampede of hooves; screeching airborne flocks sharp-clawed
      and -beaked, feathers whooshing;

skittering, slithering land beasts; the groaning, roaring she-bear.
      He's as far as he could possibly be

from camp, at the last note of his song, the last pebble. And then
      his mother's face blooms from the wall,

braids flying, shell beads clicking. He'd known without knowing that
      she would come, and knows the way out.

Mapping the Wall

51.

At first I'd cast my lines onto pages in a slow float, in slippy drifts, light-
        as-air lures making their arcs

to the watermark. A spider casts her lines and weaves. Penelope bent
        to her loom to stop time and defer

the unthinkable, all the while thinking. Now I would have to push out
        of the cave of the empty house

to find you. To let you lead me down into the spoked city's underworld,
        the packed pissy earth strewn

with broken glass and soggy condoms; to thudding nightclubs; to
        basement rooms musty with sheetless,

stained mattresses; where the ruined body, pierced, pricked with idiocy,
        the slack face and empty eyes;

other raw damaged boys, wasted . . . I closed my book and set out
        for proof you were alive.

52.

Your tags showed me you were far-famed on your own, known by self-
        monikered non-names

shifty as shadows. You were wily Odysseus slipping through Ithaca
        before going home.

He too cloaked his shoulders in rags and passed himself off as a homeless
        ghetto dweller, telling lies

to anyone who asked, *Who are you and where are you from?* just to hear
        the truth about himself.

He fooled his father, but Eurykliea who nursed him knew him *and* his
        name: "He who gives pain,"

he who calls himself No Man. What dissembled pride *you'd* feel to listen
        to a stranger tell you

about your own tag, your rumored out-of-body secret self, Zorro-esque,
        your private hero-mythogram.

53.

You knew I would come after you, apertures wide. Oh the snuffling
    snorts, the lurching, panting clatter

of me on the hunt for you! Back on the track, and what a job to tease out
    the faintest marks of you

from the clutter. Heidegger said, *the truth arises from the encounter between
    the perceiver and the object*

of perception. Much as you intended to reveal yourself, you hid from me.
    Were you CONE or COLON

or CALLIN or KALM? Each sighting, a wallop of re-knowing you, always
    a step ahead of me.

How fleet you were, sifting through the city leaving your tag, your petition
    for permanence

scribbled and folded anonymously into a crack in a blank wall, waiting
    for a god's eye. For my eye.

54.

On a map the blank spaces must be colonized and strangers replaced
      by our true familiars.

So Joshua at Jericho by divine decree bombed the walls of the ancient city,
      his nomad army armed only

with rams' horn trumpet-blasts and the shouting of the people. *Whoso*
      keeps the fig tree shall eat

the fruit thereof was reason enough. Rising or falling, a wall is a vacancy
      to adjust the viewer's angle.

For Ahab, a barnacled whale *white as wool* would be the emptiness
      on which he wrote his story.

For Rauschenberg, the erased page opened the space between himself
      and the viewer—art's aperture

into a blank field. For Banksy in Judea, a dilemma: his art perpetuates
      the occupier's wall.

55.

For two years and lack of you I snapshot your blue orthography
        and mapped your tags in the city.

The map of myself was a new world to be colonized by your marks
        like etched barcodes.

I was scannable to my fingertips. Swipe me and I'd register your
        name, whatever shape it took

on the city's geology, the Tuscarora and Oriskany sandstone in buff
        or buttery blocks, smooth or craggy;

brown Pocono, gray Pottsville in fine slabs, purplish Seneca Red;
        the Ontario greenstone of Logan Circle;

acres of ochered bricks, painted, blasted, bleached; Potomac calico
        and mottled breccia; Cockeysville marble;

Sykesville gneiss; stucco cracked, patched, spockled, painted; plain
        cinderblock; concrete . . .

56.

In only a year you were already fading. Other people caught you
and compelled you to self-erase

with a bucket and a roller. Walls fell and rose anew. Rain scoured
and the sun bleached them

blank with no help from me. Your tags one by one disappeared
like Hansel's tricky tracks

along the knotted path toward enchantment: first the white pebbles
reflecting moonlight,

then the crumbled bread. Birds will peck, snow melts, mud prints
vanish among the many,

and the red-eyed witch beckons with her gleaming teeth. I could cast
you a dreamsong

(in my dreaming helplessness) like spun lines to reel you back home,
but the walls called louder.

57.

Blank absence is still a kind of presence, said Freud. I projected myself
    at you and moved fast,

thinking that the greater my speed, the straighter my trajectory to you,
    the object and vessel

of my love for you. And so in my desire to find you, I could *receive passively*
    —as, having carried and delivered

your body, I would now receive your signs, leaned-upon by the full weight
    of you, a holy mother.

Or I could find you *narcissistically*, as when I looked into the pool of your
    beloved face over and over

in search of something familiar. *The finding of an object*, said Freud, *is
a re-finding of it*. I recognized you

in the flash of window glass, a lit puddle, a car windshield passing by,
    in the lenses of my sunglasses.

58.

Lost, Odysseus took a detour to the Underworld to get directions.
      How surprised was he

to find his mother there, Antikleia, whom last he'd seen smooth-cheeked
      and waving a yellow scarf

from her palace window as he sailed away. Now stooped, silvered,
      her voice a silken thread,

Antikleia (*antiglory*) minced no words: *it was my longing for you, your*
      cleverness and your gentle ways,

that took the sweet spirit of life from me! Three times he went to embrace
      her beloved form, but she melted

without heat or scent, without even a touch, through his arms. That's how
      ghosts are, she told him

in the fathomless black of the pit. *Strive back toward the light*, she said.
      In the end is your beginning.

59.

Lost Hansel, pecking at the gingerbread and picking at gumdrops,
    became a caged chicken

clucking for rescue by his clever sister. Odysseus, king conniver,
    penetrator of Troy's tall walls,

stepped into traps time and again and came home a dead loss, without
    men, ships or treasure.

But our hero Kilroy self-disseminates like sperm, dandelion seed, spit-
    spray, like breath—a free man.

He isn't thinking of home. He's thinking of other boys moving in packs
    through badlands and outlaw territories.

Nose to the trail I sniffed you out in Savannah and, bless your heart,
    there was your tag

big as life on Lincoln Avenue! And you? You followed your sister, hopped
    tracks and tramped away to Cali.

60.

At Dupont, I rose from black tunnels to the sweet blue breezes
      of Connecticut Avenue,

sun on the concrete street, the flower vendor and umbrella vendor
      in rainbow array. Whitman encircles us,

carved in marble: *I sit by the restless all dark night—some are so young;*
      some suffer so much—

I recall the experience sweet and sad . . . boys like you, battle fodder,
      expendable commodities,

none less than a mother's son. You've led me by the marks of your hand
      to unspool my lines to their ends,

threads that are our beginning. I hold your name in my mouth like a
      pebble. My hand filled with love

is empty. *Lord of yourself, I crown and mitre you,* under the wide sky
      and the lone crow calling.

Notes

About graffiti in Washington, DC: Roger Gastman's *Free Agents, a History of Washington DC Graffiti Art* (2001); various *Washington Post* articles about Borf, NARS, and Cool "Disco" Dan; interviews with my son.

About graffiti in general: Ernest Abel, *Painting without Permission: Toward a Psychology and Sociology of Graffiti* (1977); Banksy, *Wall and Piece* (2005) and his film "Exit through the Gift Shop" (2010); Shepard Fairey's website; Norman Mailer's groundbreaking *The Faith of Graffiti*, with photos by Jon Naar (1974, reissued in 2009); Robert Reisner, *Graffiti: 2000 Years of Wall Writing* (1971); and WK Interact, *Interior-Exterior Act 2* (2005). Films on the early days of graffiti in New York: the documentary *Style Wars* by Tony Silver and Henry Chalfant (1983); the feature *Wild Style* by Charlie Ahearn (1983); Roger Gastman and Doug Pray's feature *Infamy* (2007).

About Paleolithic cave art and art-making: B. Bowers, "Children of Prehistory," *Science News* 171 (2007); Gregory Curtis, *The Cave Painters: Probing the Mysteries of the World's First Artists* (2006); Denis Dutton, *The Art Instinct: Beauty, Pleasure and Human Evolution* (2009); R. Dale Guthrie's comprehensive *The Nature of Paleolithic Art* (2005), which argues for teenaged cave-taggers; Derek Hodgson, "Art, Perception and Information Processing: an Evolutionary Perspective," *Rock Art Research* 17, no. 1 (May 2000); Judith Thurman, "First Impressions: What Does the World's Oldest Art Say about Us?" *New Yorker*, June 23, 2008.

About hunting and tracking: Tom Brown Jr., *The Tracker* (1978); Jose Ortega y Gasset, *Meditations on Hunting* (1972); Michael Pollan's *The Omnivore's Dilemma* (2007); interviews with Jimmy Rudd and Ronnie Hines.

I'm indebted to Peter Turchi's brilliant book on mapping and writing, *Maps of the Imagination: the Writer as Car-*

tographer (2007).

You will hear lines from Dante Alighieri, "Canto XXVII," *Purgatorio,* trans. John Ciardi (1970); T. S. Eliot, "East Coker," *The Four Quartets* (1940); Zbigniew Herbert, "Pebble," *Selected Poems,* Czeslaw Milosz and Peter Dale Scott, trans. (1986); Homer, *The Odyssey of Homer,* trans. Richard Lattimore (1967); William Matthews, "Cheap Seats, the Cincinnati Gardens, Professional Basketball, 1958," *Search Party* (2004); Walt Whitman, *Leaves of Grass* (1855); Sigmund Freud, *Three Essays on the Theory of Sexuality* (1905); Martin Heidegger, *Being and Time* (1927); Bruce Chatwin, *The Songlines* (1986); and the King James Bible.

About the Author

Mary-Sherman Willis is the author of *Caveboy*, a chapbook. She is the recipient of fellowships and residencies at the Sewanee Writer's Conference, the MacDowell Colony, and the Virginia Center for the Creative Arts. Her poems and reviews have appeared in the *New Republic*, the *Hudson Review*, the *Iowa Review*, *Shenandoah*, the *Southern Poetry Review*, *Poet Lore*, online in the *Cortland Review* and *Archipelago.org*, and other journals. Her poems have been featured in Ted Kooser's *American Life in Poetry* and in several anthologies. She is a graduate of the Warren Wilson Program for Writers, lives in Virginia, and teaches at George Washington University.

CPSIA information can be obtained at www.ICGtesting.com
Printed in the USA
BVOW02s1524181213

339184BV00001B/15/P